FAST AND FURIOUS

D0317915

LIVEWIRE WARRINGTON	
34143101314613	
Bertrams	24/06/2013
JN	£7.99
WAR	

An Hachette UK Company
www.hachette.co.uk

First published in Great Britain in 2013 by TickTock, an imprint of Octopus
Publishing Group Ltd
Endeavour House
189 Shaftesbury Avenue
London
WC2H 8JY
www.octopusbooks.co.uk

Copyright © Octopus Publishing Group Ltd 2013

All rights reserved. No part of this work may be reproduced or utilised in
any form or by any means, electronic or mechanical, including photocopying,
recording or by any information storage and retrieval system, without the prior
written permission of the publisher.

ISBN 978 1 84898 821 7
A CIP catalogue record for this book is available from the British Library

Printed and bound in China

10 9 8 7 6 5 4 3 2 1

Picture credits:
b=bottom; c=centre; t=top; r=right; l=left

Alamy 75t, 85t; Aviation Picture Library: 12-15, 20-21, 24-27; Beken of Cowes
76-77c, 80-81c; Car Photo Library – carphoto.co.uk 6, 40-69; Bill Scott 84-85c;
Corbis 30-31, 81t, 90-91c; Hawkes Ocean Technologies 91t; iStockphoto.com
28-29; Jane's Defence Weekly 88-89c; John Clark Photography 72-73;
Lockheed 7t, 18-19; Nasa 8-11, 22-23; RNLI 7b, 78-79, 86-87; Shutterstock front
cover, 1, 38-39; Skyscan 16-17; Stena 74-75c; US Coast Guard 32-35, 89t

Every effort has been made to trace the copyright holders, and we apologise
in advance for any unintentional omissions. We would be pleased to insert the
appropriate acknowledgments in any subsequent edition of this publication.

Contents

Introduction

Fast and Furious showcases some of the fastest and most powerful vehicles ever made, in three thrilling sections: In the Air, On Land and On the Water.

In the Air

Discover the most impressive aircraft of the past fifty years, from the Space Shuttle, entrusted with 135 missions, to top-secret military planes like the Lockheed SR-71 Blackbird and the stealth bomber B2-Spirit. Plus commercial jetliners like the legendary *Concorde* and the Airbus A380 that can carry nearly 1,000 passengers.

On Land

Marvel at the most phenomenal cars and bikes ever built, including classic vehicles unsurpassed in speed and design. Find out about the Aston Martin V12 Vanquish,

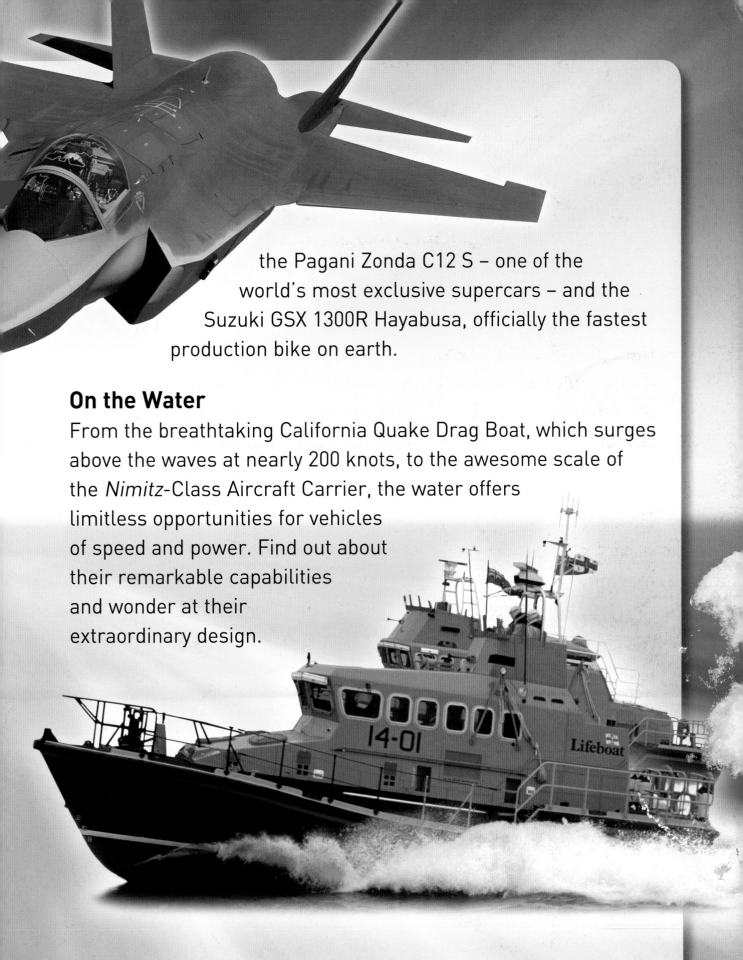

the Pagani Zonda C12 S – one of the world's most exclusive supercars – and the Suzuki GSX 1300R Hayabusa, officially the fastest production bike on earth.

On the Water

From the breathtaking California Quake Drag Boat, which surges above the waves at nearly 200 knots, to the awesome scale of the *Nimitz*-Class Aircraft Carrier, the water offers limitless opportunities for vehicles of speed and power. Find out about their remarkable capabilities and wonder at their extraordinary design.

In the Air

This section is dedicated to every type of aircraft, from the Space Shuttle, the first real spacecraft to be brought back to Earth, to military planes, like the monster eight engine B-52 Stratofortress – the fighter pilots' 'Big Ugly Fat Fellow' – which will keep flying at least until 2040. Then there is the iconic, streamlined and superfast *Concorde*, which was once the world's fastest passenger jetliner, and vital rescue craft like the P-3 Orion Firefighting Airtanker and the Jayhawk helicopter, whose speed and power are essential for emergency intervention and to assist those stranded at sea.

F-117A Nighthawk

First flown in 1981, the F-117A could be the weirdest aircraft ever made. Its shape was designed to break up enemy radar signals. Because it could be refuelled in midair, the F-117A was able to fly almost anywhere. Retired in 2008, this amazing plane was made by the US company Lockheed.

Three Nighthawks are on display in the US. At the United States Air Force Museum visitors can walk right up to this incredible aircraft.

DID YOU KNOW?
Nighthawk pilots called themselves 'Bandits'.

26

DID YOU KNOW?

Stacks of brilliant facts to really impress your friends! For example, did you know that as the X-43 A reaches supersonic speeds some of its metal parts melt from the intense heat? And there's more...

The F-117A was a bomber plane. Its zigzag-shaped doors opened and shut very quickly to release bombs.

The hundreds of flat surfaces on the plane made it almost invisible on radar.

STATS & FACTS

All key data at your fingertips, to help you compare military aircraft and commercial jetliners: from launch date, model and range to top speed, weight, wing span, crew and passenger capacity. See which is the fastest and which the most powerful!

STATS & FACTS

LAUNCHED: 1981

RETIRED: 2008

ORIGIN: US

MODELS: FIVE PROTOTYPES AND 59 PRODUCTION AIRCRAFT

ENGINES: TWO GENERAL ELECTRIC F404-F1D2 TURBOFANS, EACH GIVING 4,899 KG THRUST

WINGSPAN: 13.2 M

LENGTH: 20.08 M

COCKPIT CREW: ONE

MAXIMUM SPEED: MACH 1 (993 KM/H / 617 MPH)

MAXIMUM WEIGHT: 23.4 TONNES

RANGE: WITHOUT AIR REFUELLING, ABOUT 2,400 KM (1,500 MILES)

LOAD: TWO LASER-GUIDED BOMBS

COST: £23.6 MILLION

27

Space Shuttle

Early space flights relied on rockets – giant tubes fired into orbit. The Space Shuttle was the first spacecraft that could be brought back to Earth. NASA used it on 135 missions from 1981 to 2011, when it was retired.

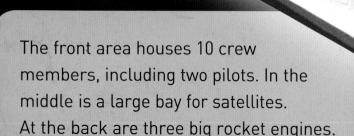

The front area houses 10 crew members, including two pilots. In the middle is a large bay for satellites. At the back are three big rocket engines.

DID YOU KNOW?

The Shuttle's boosters fall off into the ocean. They are recovered and used again.

Heat-resistant tiles protect the Shuttle when it returns to Earth. It glides onto a runway and is slowed down by a big parachute.

The orbiter is attached to a huge tank holding liquid oxygen and liquid hydrogen. A solid rocket booster is on each side.

STATS & FACTS

LAUNCHED: 1981

ORIGIN: US

MODELS: *DISCOVERY, ATLANTIS, ENDEAVOUR, COLUMBIA, CHALLENGER*

ENGINES: THREE ORBITER ENGINES THAT EACH PRODUCE A VACUUM THRUST OF 213,188 KG

WINGSPAN: 23.79 M

LENGTH: 37.24 M

CREW: UP TO 10

MAXIMUM SPEED: 28,164 KM/H (17,500 MPH)

MAXIMUM LANDING WEIGHT: 100 TONNES

RANGE: 187-643 KM (116-403 MILES)

LOAD: SATELLITES, COMPONENTS FOR THE JOINT SPACE STATION AND SPACE EXPERIMENTS

COST: £1.05 BILLION, PLUS £278 MILLION FOR EACH LAUNCH

X-43A

NASA (National Aeronautics and Space Administration) is best known for space exploration, but it also conducts important research into aircraft. The X-43A is one of the latest research planes. It is a hypersonic (faster than Mach 5) plane that flies without a pilot.

Guinness World Records recognised the X-43A Scramjet with a world speed record for a jet-powered aircraft – an amazing Mach 9.6!

DID YOU KNOW?

At high Mach speeds the heat is so great that metal portions of the plane's frame melt.

The X-43A's first flight took place on 2nd June 2001.
It was dropped from a B-52 over the Pacific Ocean.
However, the plane broke up in the sky.

The X-43A has a wide bottom, flat top and two fins. Its Scramjet engine burns hydrogen-based fuel.

STATS & FACTS

LAUNCHED: 2001 (TEST VERSION)

ORIGIN: US

MODELS: X-43A, X-43B, X-43C, X-43D

ENGINE: GASL HYDROGEN-FUELLED SCRAMJET ENGINE

WINGSPAN: 1.5 M

LENGTH: 3.66 M

CREW: UNMANNED AT PRESENT

MAXIMUM SPEED: MACH 10 (10,622 KM/H / 6,600 MPH)

MAXIMUM WEIGHT: 1.3 TONNES

RANGE: UNKNOWN

COST: £150 MILLION

SR-71 Blackbird

In 1960, the Soviet Union shot down an American spy plane. After this disaster the US government hired Lockheed Corporation to build a craft that would never be shot down. The result was the amazing SR-71, packed with cameras and sensors. Despite its dangerous missions, not one of the 32 Blackbirds built was lost in combat.

Nicknamed 'Blackbird' because of its dark colour, the plane is made of titanium alloy, which protects it from the extreme heat produced by flying at Mach 3.

DID YOU KNOW?

The SR-71 flight manual contains over 1,000 pages and is available online.

The Blackbird was top secret. President Lyndon Johnson didn't even admit it existed until six months after its maiden flight in 1964.

Large spikes keep the plane balanced.

STATS & FACTS

LAUNCHED: 1966

RETIRED: 1998

ORIGIN: US

MODELS: SR-71A, SR-71B; OTHER VARIANTS INCLUDE THE A-12, YF-12A, M-21 AND D-21 DRONE

ENGINES: TWO PRATT & WHITNEY J58-P-10S WITH AFTERBURNERS

WINGSPAN: 16.94 M

LENGTH: 31.65 M

COCKPIT CREW: TWO

MAXIMUM SPEED: MACH 3 (3,500 KM/H / 2,200 MPH)

MAXIMUM WEIGHT: 64 TONNES

RANGE: 5,400 KM (3,300 MILES)

LOAD: SENSORS AND CAMERAS

COST: £33 MILLION TO BUILD; £30,000 AN HOUR TO FLY

Eurofighter Typhoon

Four European countries – Germany, Italy, Spain and the UK – developed this warplane together. Typhoons are built on four separate assembly lines, with each country building its own national aircraft.

Only 15 per cent of the Eurofighter's body is metal. The rest is mainly lightweight carbon fibre, which keeps the plane from overheating.

DID YOU KNOW?

By January 2011, Typhoons in service since 2003 had flown over 100,000 hours.

The twin engines allow the Typhoon to accelerate to Mach 1 – the speed of sound – in under 30 seconds. The Typhoon also takes off in just 5 seconds!

The Typhoon has a large triangular wing and small powered foreplanes on each side of the nose.

STATS & FACTS

LAUNCHED: 2002

ORIGIN: EUROPE

MODELS: TWIN-ENGINE, CANARD-DELTA WING MULTIROLE AIRCRAFT ENGINES: TWO EUROJET EJ200 REHEATED TURBOFANS EACH PROVIDING 9,072 KG THRUST

WINGSPAN: 10.95 M

LENGTH: 15.96 M

COCKPIT CREW: ONE OR TWO

MAXIMUM SPEED: MACH 2 (2,495 KM/H / 1,550 MPH)

MAXIMUM WEIGHT: 23.5 TONNES

RANGE: 2,900 KM (1,800 MILES)

LOAD: GUNS, MISSILES, BOMBS

COST: £65 MILLION

Concorde

In 1962, Britain and France joined forces to build a supersonic commercial aircraft – *Concorde*.
First flown in 1969, *Concorde* entered service in 1976 and flew for 27 years before being retired.
Cruising at Mach 2 – twice the speed of sound – this amazing plane made the trip from London to New York in just over three hours.

Concorde's slim body and paper-dart shape enabled it to fly more than twice as fast as other passenger planes.

DID YOU KNOW?

Twenty *Concordes* were built. Five are now on show in museums.

Concorde's entire nose hinged down so the pilot could see when landing.

Concorde's four powerful engines allowed the plane to reach 363 km/h (225 mph) in just 30 seconds.

STATS & FACTS

LAUNCHED: 1969

ORIGIN: FRANCE AND THE UK

MODELS: ONLY ONE PRODUCTION TYPE, WHICH IS LARGER THAN PROTOTYPES

ENGINES: FOUR ROLLS-ROYCE/ SNECMA OLYMPUS S93 TURBOJETS, PROVIDING 17,260 KG THRUST

WINGSPAN: 25.6 M

LENGTH: 61.66 M

COCKPIT CREW: TWO PILOTS

MAXIMUM SPEED: MACH 2 (2,173 KM/H / 1,350 MPH)

MAXIMUM WEIGHT: 185 TONNES

RANGE: 7,242 KM (4,500 MILES)

LOAD: ROOM FOR 140 PASSENGERS, BUT USUALLY SEATED 100

COST: £23 MILLION (IN 1977); THIS WOULD BE ABOUT £200 MILLION TODAY

Joint Strike Fighter

In 1995, the US Air Force and US Navy launched a programme for a JSF (Joint Strike Fighter). The goal was to produce the next generation of planes for airfields and aircraft carriers.

All JSFs carry weapons on each side of the fuselage.

DID YOU KNOW?

The JSF will replace fighter, strike and ground attack aircraft for the US, UK, Canada, Australia, and their allies.

There are three versions of the JSF. The F-35A is the basic version. The F-35B has a more powerful engine. The F-35C (right) has a bigger wing, which can fold.

The rear exhaust produces thrust to lift the aircraft.

STATS & FACTS

LAUNCHED: 1995

ORIGIN: US

MODELS: F-35A, F-35B, AND F-35C

ENGINES: ONE PRATT & WHITNEY F135 TURBOFAN OR ONE F136 GE TURBOFAN; FOR THE F-35B, ONE F135 PRATT & WHITNEY TURBOFAN OR ONE F136 GE TURBOFAN AND ROLLS-ROYCE ALLISON ENGINE-DRIVEN LIFT FAN, DELIVERING 11, 340 KG AND 8,164 KG THRUST

WINGSPAN: UP TO 13.1 M

LENGTH: UP TO 15.5 M

COCKPIT CREW: ONE

MAXIMUM SPEED: MACH 1.8 (1,900 KM/H / 1,200 MPH)

MAXIMUM WEIGHT: 22.7 TONNES

RANGE: ABOUT 2,200 KM (1,380 MILES)

LOAD: ENORMOUS VARIETY OF GUNS, MISSILES AND BOMBS

COST: £57 MILLION

Harrier

By the late 1950s, air forces wanted planes that could operate from car parks, forest clearings, or even small ships. Hawker Aircraft in the UK launched one of the first VTOL (Vertical Take-off and Landing) aircraft in 1969. This plane is the Harrier. It is also known as the 'Jump Jet'.

DID YOU KNOW?

The US Marine Corps uses the Harrier to provide air power for forces invading an enemy shore.

This single-seat Sea Harrier operates from aircraft carriers. There are also two-seater and training versions.

Harriers have a system called VIFF (Vectoring in Forward Flight) that lets them perform tricky manoeuvres.

STATS & FACTS

LAUNCHED: 1969

ORIGIN: UK

MODELS: ELEVEN VERSIONS

ENGINES: ONE ROLLS-ROYCE PEGASUS 6 OR 11, DEPENDING ON THE VERSION; THE VECTORED THRUST TURBOFAN PROVIDES 6,800 KG TO 10,660 KG THRUST, DEPENDING ON THE VERSION

WINGSPAN: UP TO 9.25 M

LENGTH: UP TO 14.5 M

COCKPIT CREW: ONE TO TWO

MAXIMUM SPEED: MACH 1 (1,180 KM/H / 735 MPH)

MAXIMUM WEIGHT: UP TO 14 TONNES

RANGE: WITHOUT AIR REFUELLING, ABOUT 2,736 KM (1,700 MILES)

LOAD: MISSILES, ROCKETS, BOMBS

COST: £14.5 TO 18.5 MILLION

The engine has two nozzles on each side. They blast downward for take-off and forward to slow down.

B-2 Spirit

Stealth airplanes are designed to avoid detection by enemy radar. First flown in 1989, the B-2 stealth bomber looks like it came from another planet.

B-2 technology comes at a price – each plane costs an amazing £716 million!

The strange bulges in the B-2 hide its engines, cockpit and bombs.

DID YOU KNOW?

The B-2's skin is jet-black and smooth and all joints are hidden.

The plane has just two crew members: a pilot and a mission commander. The rest of the cockpit contains computer-controlled flight equipment.

STATS & FACTS

LAUNCHED: 1989

ORIGIN: US

MODELS: THE US AIR FORCE HAS 20 PLANES, ALL SLIGHTLY DIFFERENT

ENGINES: FOUR GENERAL ELECTRIC F118-GE-100 ENGINES, EACH WITH A THRUST OF 7,850 KG

WINGSPAN: 52 M

LENGTH: 21 M

COCKPIT CREW: TWO

MAXIMUM SPEED: HIGH SUBSONIC

MAXIMUM WEIGHT: 181 TONNES

RANGE: INTERCONTINENTAL

LOAD: CONVENTIONAL OR NUCLEAR WEAPONS

COST: £716 MILLION

F-117A Nighthawk

First flown in 1981, the F-117A could be the weirdest aircraft ever made. Its shape was designed to break up enemy radar signals. Because it could be refuelled in midair, the F-117A was able to fly almost anywhere. Retired in 2008, this amazing plane was made by the US company Lockheed.

Three Nighthawks are on display in the US. At the United States Air Force Museum visitors can walk right up to this incredible aircraft.

DID YOU KNOW?

Nighthawk pilots called themselves 'Bandits'.

The F-117A was a bomber plane. Its zigzag-shaped doors opened and shut very quickly to release bombs.

The hundreds of flat surfaces on the plane made it almost invisible on radar.

STATS & FACTS

LAUNCHED: 1981

RETIRED: 2008

ORIGIN: US

MODELS: FIVE PROTOTYPES AND 59 PRODUCTION AIRCRAFT

ENGINES: TWO GENERAL ELECTRIC F404-F1D2 TURBOFANS, EACH GIVING 4,899 KG THRUST

WINGSPAN: 13.2 M

LENGTH: 20.08 M

COCKPIT CREW: ONE

MAXIMUM SPEED: MACH 1 (993 KM/H / 617 MPH)

MAXIMUM WEIGHT: 23.4 TONNES

RANGE: WITHOUT AIR REFUELLING, ABOUT 2,400 KM (1,500 MILES)

LOAD: TWO LASER-GUIDED BOMBS

COST: £23.6 MILLION

Airbus A380

Ever since the first plane took to the skies, aircraft have become bigger and bigger. In 2007, European manufacturer Airbus introduced the largest commercial aircraft to date: the enormous Airbus A380.

This gentle giant is the quietest wide-body jetliner in the air. It generates 50 per cent less noise than its nearest competitor.

DID YOU KNOW?

During take-off the wings of the A380 flex upward by over 4 metres.

The double-decker A380 can carry up to 853 passengers.

The A380 includes open spaces and social areas. The interiors can be custom-designed. Singapore Airlines' A380s include separate sitting and sleeping areas, complete with full-sized beds!

STATS & FACTS

LAUNCHED: 2007

ORIGIN: EUROPE (SPECIFICALLY FRANCE, GERMANY, SPAIN AND THE UK)

MODELS: A380-800 PASSENGER PLANE; A380-800F FOR CARGO

ENGINES: TWO NEW-GENERATION ENGINE OPTIONS: THE ENGINE ALLIANCE GP7200 AND ROLLS-ROYCE TRENT 900

WINGSPAN: 79.8 M

LENGTH: 72.75 M

COCKPIT CREW: TWO

SEATING: UP TO 853

MAXIMUM SPEED: 945 KM/H (588 MPH)

MAXIMUM WEIGHT: 569 TONNES FOR TAKE-OFF

RANGE: 14,800 KM (9,200 MILES)

LOAD: UP TO 853 PASSENGERS OR 150 TONNES OF CARGO

COST: ABOUT £155 MILLION

P-3 Orion Firefighting Airtanker

P-3 Airtankers are old military aircraft that were originally developed as spy planes. They were adapted for civilian use and are now used to fight forest fires. They carry massive amounts of fire retardant, which is dropped on the blaze below.

DID YOU KNOW?

The Orion is named after a group of stars called Orion, the Great Hunter.

The P-3 used for firefighting has low wings and four turbine engines with four-blade propellers.

Computer-controlled doors under the body of the plane open to drop the retardant.

The fire retardant is dropped in a line, which acts as a barrier to stop the fire from spreading.

STATS & FACTS

LAUNCHED (AS AIRTANKER): 1990

ORIGIN: US

MAXIMUM POWER: 2,500 BHP

LENGTH: 35.6 M

WINGSPAN: NEARLY 30 M

HEIGHT: 11.8 M

MAXIMUM SPEED: 657 KM/H (411 MPH)

RETARDANT TANK CAPACITY: 11,356 LITRES

MAXIMUM LOAD: 20 TONNES

WEIGHT: 43.4 TONNES

MAXIMUM TAKEOFF WEIGHT: 63.4 TONNES

TAKEOFF RUN REQUIRED: 1,300 M

CREW: 15

On Land

The swiftest, most powerful and iconic two- and four-wheel vehicles ever to hit the road are the stars of this section. They're classic, stylish, but most of all fast! Marvel at the elegant Bugatti Veyron 16.4, which could fly off the tarmac at 400 km/h if it weren't for the clever Formula One aerodynamics, or the rather unique $1 million dollar McLaren F1, with its distinctive butterfly doors and central driving position. No less impressive are the 'king of all sports bikes', the Ninja ZX-14, which with its 1,441 cc engine is the most powerful production bike ever, and the Suzuki GSX 1300R Hayabusa, officially the fastest bike on earth!

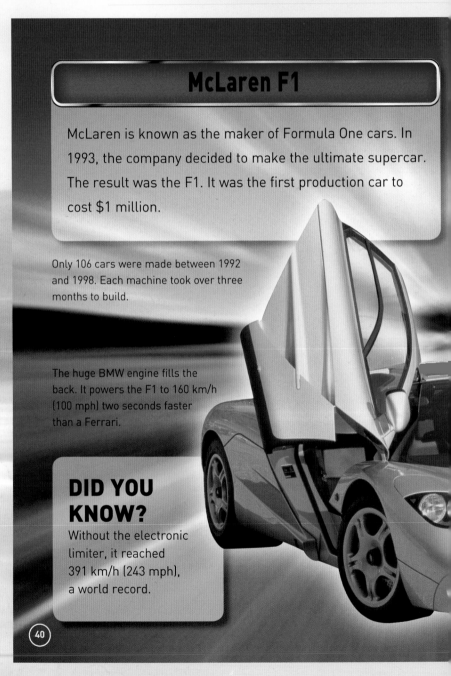

McLaren F1

McLaren is known as the maker of Formula One cars. In 1993, the company decided to make the ultimate supercar. The result was the F1. It was the first production car to cost $1 million.

Only 106 cars were made between 1992 and 1998. Each machine took over three months to build.

The huge BMW engine fills the back. It powers the F1 to 160 km/h (100 mph) two seconds faster than a Ferrari.

DID YOU KNOW?

Without the electronic limiter, it reached 391 km/h (243 mph), a world record.

40

DID YOU KNOW?

Mine these nuggets of knowledge to give you the edge over your mates! Who would have guessed that a turbo-charged Blackbird could do a wheelie at 320 km/h or that buying a Pagani Zonda entitled you to a free pair of driving shoes, made by the Pope's shoemaker! It doesn't get more exclusive than that! And there's more...

The central driving position is unusual for a sports car. So are the two rear seats.

STATS & FACTS

STATS & FACTS

LAUNCHED: 1993

ORIGIN: UK

ENGINE: 6,064 CC 48-VALVE V12, MID-MOUNTED

MAXIMUM POWER: 627 BHP AT 7,400 RPM

MAXIMUM TORQUE: 479 LB PER FT AT 7,000 RPM

MAXIMUM SPEED: 386 KM/H (240 MPH)

ACCELERATION:
0-100 KM/H (60 MPH) IN 3.2 SECONDS
0-160 KM/H (100 MPH) IN 6.3 SECONDS

WEIGHT: 1.14 TONNES

COST: £634,700

41

All key data at your fingertips, to help you compare engine size, power, torque, speed and acceleration of the best cars and bikes on land, and discover which is the fastest and which the most powerful! Buckle up, rev up and feel the power!

Bugatti Veyron 16.4

Volkswagen bought the legendary brand Bugatti in 1998 and launched the Veyron in 2003. A new model was produced in 2005. Inspired by the old Bugattis, it featured F1 safety technology so that the car could safely top 400 km/h (250 mph). It is so fast, it would lift off the ground if it weren't for the clever aerodynamics.

DID YOU KNOW?

A special edition Veyron 16.4 was created in collaboration with the fashion house Hermès. Unveiled at the 2008 Geneva Motor Show, it is so special it costs £1.5 million!

Ceramic brakes stop the car faster than it accelerates. It stops in 2.3 seconds from 100km/h (60 mph)!

The interior of the Bugatti Veyron 16.4 had to feel elegant, luxurious, and classic, while featuring the most modern technology.

To be fast, the Veyron 16.4 must be light. It is made from the lowest weight materials, including titanium, carbon and aluminium.

STATS & FACTS

LAUNCHED: 2005

ORIGIN: FRANCE

ENGINE: 8.0L W16-CYLINDER, QUAD TURBOCHARGER

MAXIMUM POWER: 1,001 BHP

MAXIMUM TORQUE: 1,922 LB PER FT AT 2,200–5,500 RPM

MAXIMUM SPEED: 407 KM/H (253 MPH)

ACCELERATION: 0-100 KM/H (0-60 MPH) IN 2.5 SECONDS

WEIGHT: 1,888 KG

COST: £1,087,000 (BASIC PRICE)

McLaren F1

McLaren is known as the maker of Formula One cars. In 1993, the company decided to make the ultimate supercar. The result was the F1. It was the first production car to cost $1 million.

Only 106 cars were made between 1992 and 1998. Each machine took over three months to build.

The huge BMW engine fills the back. It powers the F1 to 160 km/h (100 mph) two seconds faster than a Ferrari.

DID YOU KNOW?

Without the electronic limiter, it reached 391 km/h (243 mph), a world record.

The central driving position is unusual for a sports car. So are the two rear seats.

STATS & FACTS

LAUNCHED: 1993

ORIGIN: UK

ENGINE: 6,064 CC 48-VALVE V12, MID-MOUNTED

MAXIMUM POWER: 627 BHP AT 7,400 RPM

MAXIMUM TORQUE: 479 LB PER FT AT 7,000 RPM

MAXIMUM SPEED: 386 KM/H (240 MPH)

ACCELERATION:
0-100 KM/H (60 MPH) IN 3.2 SECONDS
0-160 KM/H (100 MPH) IN 6.3 SECONDS

WEIGHT: 1.14 TONNES

COST: £634,700

Pagani Zonda C12 S

This car was designed by Horacio Pagani, who is from Argentina. It is named after a wind that blows from the Andes Mountains. The Pagani Zonda is perhaps the most exclusive supercar. Approximately 25 Zondas are built per year.

This C12 S model has a massive V12 engine.

If you drive a Zonda you have to travel light. The car doesn't have a boot!

DID YOU KNOW?

When you buy a Zonda, you get a pair of driving shoes made by the Pope's shoemaker.

The Zonda looks like a fighter plane. It has a glass-roofed cabin and twin spoilers. The inside is made of aluminium, suede, leather and carbon fibre.

STATS & FACTS

LAUNCHED: 2001

ORIGIN: ITALY

ENGINE: 7,010 CC V12, MID-MOUNTED

MAXIMUM POWER: 562 BHP AT 5,500 RPM

MAXIMUM TORQUE: 553 LB PER FT AT 4,100 RPM

MAXIMUM SPEED: 354 KM/H (220 MPH)

ACCELERATION: 0-100 KM/H (0-60 MPH) IN 3.7 SECONDS

WEIGHT: 1.25 TONNES

COST: £298,000

Jaguar XJ220S

In the late 1980s, British carmaker Jaguar built a supercar called the XJ220. The car was delivered in 1992 and its price was £415,000. Two years later, Jaguar produced a faster, lighter and cheaper version, the XJ220S.

The spoiler stretched across one of the widest sports cars ever made.

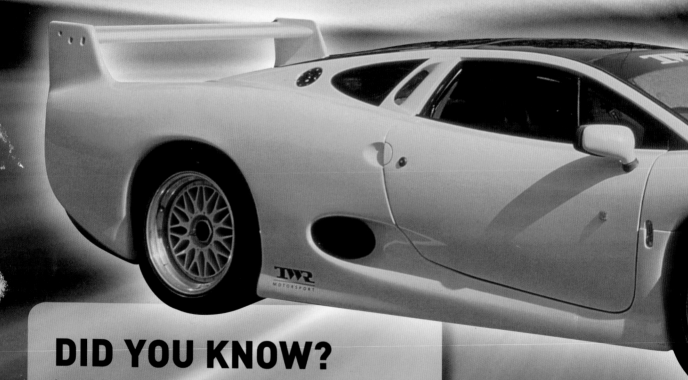

DID YOU KNOW?

In 1994, racing-car driver Martin Brundle reached 347 km/h (217 mph) in an XJ220S – at the time a record for a production car.

The XJ220S was built by TWR (Tom Walkinshaw Racing). The design was based on the XJ220C cars that took part in the Le Mans race in France in 1993.

STATS & FACTS

LAUNCHED: 1992

ORIGIN: UK

ENGINE: 3,498 CC TWIN-TURBO V6, MID-MOUNTED

MAXIMUM POWER: 680 BHP AT 7,200 RPM

MAXIMUM TORQUE: 527 LB PER FT AT 5,000 RPM

MAXIMUM SPEED: 350 KM/H (217 MPH)

ACCELERATION: 0-60 MPH (0-100 KM/H) IN 3.3 SECONDS

WEIGHT: 1.08 TONNES

COST: £293,750

The XJ220's aluminium body was replaced with carbon fibre to make the XJ220S even lighter.

Lamborghini Murciélago

Ferruccio Lamborghini was a wealthy Italian tractor maker. Unhappy with his Ferrari, he decided to build a better car. In 1966, Lamborghini made the first supercar, the Miura. In 2001, the company introduced the Murciélago. Production of the Murciélago ended in 2010. Its successor, the Aventador, was released in 2011.

DID YOU KNOW?

The Lamborghini logo is a charging bull. The Murciélago was named after a bull that fought so well in a bullring in Spain that its life was spared.

To reverse the Murciélago, most drivers flip open a door and sit on the edge of the car so they can look over their shoulders!

The roof and the doors of the Murciélago are made of steel. The rest of the car is made of carbon fibre.

STATS & FACTS

LAUNCHED: 2001

ORIGIN: ITALY

ENGINE: 6,192 CC V12, MID-MOUNTED

MAXIMUM POWER: 571 BHP AT 7,500 RPM

MAXIMUM TORQUE: 479 LB PER FT AT 5,400 RPM

MAXIMUM SPEED: 330 KM/H (205 MPH)

ACCELERATION: 0-60 MPH (0-100 KM/H) IN 4 SECONDS

WEIGHT: 1.65 TONNES

COST: FROM £163,000

The Murciélago has four-wheel drive and a safety system that slows the car down if it starts to lose its grip on the road.

Ferrari F50

Ferrari makes some of the finest sports cars in the world. The F50 is one of the most exclusive models ever built. Just 349 cars were produced between 1995 and 1997 to celebrate the Italian legend's 50th anniversary. This incredible car boasted a slightly less powerful version of a 1989 Formula One engine.

DID YOU KNOW?

The F50 was very expensive. But you still had to roll the windows up and down by hand!

Underneath the car, the body is completely flat. The four exhausts stick out through holes cut into the rear, like a racing car.

The F50's body, doors and seats are made from lightweight carbon fibre.

The engine is in the middle of the F50. It powers the Ferrari to 100 km/h (60 mph) in under 4 seconds.

STATS & FACTS

LAUNCHED: 1995

ORIGIN: ITALY

ENGINE: 4,699 CC 60-VALVE V12, MID-MOUNTED

MAXIMUM POWER: 520 BHP AT 8,500 RPM

MAXIMUM TORQUE: 347 LB PER FT AT 6,500 RPM

MAXIMUM SPEED: 325 KM/H (202 MPH)

ACCELERATION: 0-60 MPH (0-100 KM/H) IN 3.7 SECONDS

WEIGHT: 1.23 TONNES

COST: AROUND £342,700

Porsche 911 GT2

From the outside the GT2 looks like an ordinary Porsche 911 Turbo. But inside all of the luxuries have been removed to make it run like a racing car. The car has harder suspension, a roll cage, special brakes and lots of extra power!

DID YOU KNOW?

A GTS RS variant went on sale in 2010. It could top 330 km/h (205 mph). Only 500 cars were available in the US, and they sold out within hours.

The GT2 is 10 per cent more powerful and 7 per cent lighter than the 911 Turbo.

The spoiler and side panels have vents that cool the huge engine. There are also slats in the bonnet.

The GT2 accelerates to 298 km/h (186 mph) and brakes to a stop in less than 60 seconds.

STATS & FACTS

LAUNCHED: 2001

ORIGIN: GERMANY

ENGINE: 3,600 CC 24-VALVE TURBO FLAT 6, REAR-MOUNTED

MAXIMUM POWER: 455 BHP AT 5,700 RPM

MAXIMUM TORQUE: 459 LB PER FT AT 3,500 RPM

MAXIMUM SPEED: 317 KM/H (197 MPH)

ACCELERATION: 0-100 KM/H (0-62 MPH) IN 4.1 SECONDS

WEIGHT: 1.44 TONNES

COST: £110,000

TVR Tuscan

The TVR Tuscan is a sports car that was manufactured in the United Kingdom from 2000 to 2006. The car was made as light as possible and had a huge engine. As a result, it was amazingly fast and cost less than its rivals.

DID YOU KNOW?

John Travolta drove a purple Tuscan in the 2001 movie *Swordfish*.

To get into the Tuscan, drivers pressed a button under the sideview mirror. To get out, they twisted a knob in the car.

The roof and rear window could be removed and stored in the boot. There was even space left over for suitcases!

The engine filled most of the space under the bonnet.

STATS & FACTS

LAUNCHED: 2000

ORIGIN: UK

ENGINE: 3,605 CC 24 VALVE INLINE 6, FRONT-MOUNTED

MAXIMUM POWER: 350 BHP AT 7,200 RPM

MAXIMUM TORQUE: 290 LB PER FT AT 5,500 RPM

MAXIMUM SPEED: 290 KM/H (180 MPH)

ACCELERATION: 0-100 KM/H (0-60 MPH) IN 4.4 SECONDS

WEIGHT: 1.1 TONNES

COST: £40,000

Kawasaki Ninja ZX-12R

The Japanese company Kawasaki has always made very fast motorcycles. Produced from 2000 to 2006, the ZX-12R was one of the fastest bikes on the planet, capable of just under 320 km/h (200 mph). The Ninja also had a big fuel tank, so it could travel long distances.

The ZX-12R could go from 113 km/h (70 mph) to a complete stop in under 4 seconds.

DID YOU KNOW?

The ZX-12R had the widest back tyre of any sports bike. It was a huge 20 cm wide!

The scoop under the headlight forced air into the engine, which dragged extra fuel in. This gave the ZX-12R even more power.

In 2012, the 'king of all sports bikes' was launched. With a 1,441 cc engine, the Ninja ZX-14 is the most powerful production bike ever made.

STATS & FACTS

LAUNCHED: 2000

ORIGIN: JAPAN

ENGINE: 1,199 CC

CYLINDERS: 4

MAXIMUM POWER: 165 BHP AT 9,800 RPM

MAXIMUM TORQUE: 130 NM AT 7,800 RPM

GEARS: 6

DRY WEIGHT: 210 KG

MAXIMUM SPEED: 305.8 KM/H (190 MPH)

FUEL TANK CAPACITY: 20 LITRES

COLOURS: BLACK/GOLD, SILVER, KAWASAKI GREEN

COST: £9,500

Suzuki GSX 1300R Hayabusa

The Japanese manufacturer Suzuki was founded in 1952. In 1998, it built a superfast motorcycle called the Hayabusa. In 2000, new safety regulations limited the speed of all new bikes. This model is officially the fastest production bike on Earth, since no other motorcycle can be made to go faster without being altered.

The British Land Speed Record for a motorcycle is held by a turbo-charged Hayabusa. It topped 388 km/h (241 mph)!

DID YOU KNOW?

A Hayabusa is so powerful that it can wear out a back tyre in as little as 1,600 km (1,000 miles).

This is the Hayabusa 2011.
Powered by a 1340 cc,
16-valve engine, it is one
of the fastest sport bikes
currently in production.

The Hayabusa is a bird of prey that eats blackbirds. Suzuki
named its new bike Hayabusa because
it was faster and more powerful than
Honda's Blackbird, its rival.

STATS & FACTS

LAUNCHED: 1998

ORIGIN: JAPAN

ENGINE: 1,298 CC

CYLINDERS: 4

MAXIMUM POWER: 155 BHP
AT 9,000 RPM

MAXIMUM TORQUE: 134 NM
AT 6,800 RPM

GEARS: 6

DRY WEIGHT: 215 KG

MAX SPEED: 299 KM/H (186 MPH)

FUEL TANK CAPACITY: 18 LITRES

COLOURS: BLUE & BLACK, BLUE &
SILVER, SILVER

COST: £8,299

Ducati 999S

Ducati is an Italian motorcycle company that was bought by the German car manufacturer Audi in 2012. The 999 was the fastest and most expensive motorcycle Ducati produced. It was made of carbon fibre and aluminium.

The seat and fuel tank could be moved backward and forward, and the footrests moved up and down. This Ducati was comfortable to ride, whatever your height.

DID YOU KNOW?

The Ducati 999S was capable of reaching 100 km/h (62 mph) in under three seconds.

This is the Ducati 1199 Panigale. The name links the bike to its origins in Borgo Panigale, near Bologna, Italy. The area is called 'Motor Valley'.

The 999 range enjoyed great success in the Superbike World Championship and was raced through the 2007 season, despite no longer being produced.

STATS & FACTS

LAUNCHED: 2006

ORIGIN: ITALY

ENGINE: 998 CC

CYLINDERS: 2

MAXIMUM POWER: 143 BHP AT 10,000 RPM

MAXIMUM TORQUE: 111.8 NM AT 8,000 RPM

GEARS: 6

DRY WEIGHT: 186 KG

MAX SPEED: 281.6 KM/H (175 MPH)

FUEL TANK CAPACITY: 15.5 LITRES

COLOURS: RED OR BLACK

COST: £19,300

Yamaha YZF R1

Originally a maker of musical instruments, Yamaha started making motorcycles after World War II. In 2009, Yamaha produced a new version of its open-class sport bike, the YZF R1. The engine technology came from the M1 Moto GP bike driven by Valentino Rossi, with its cross-plane crankshaft and irregular firing intervals.

DID YOU KNOW?

A new throttle control allows the rider to choose between three distinct modes, depending on the rider's environment.

A subframe in magnesium cast in a carbon fibre mould makes the bike both strong and light.

In previous models the dual projector headlights were integrated with the air induction intakes. This accentuated the aerodynamic look and gave the bike an aggressive image.

STATS & FACTS

LAUNCHED: 2009

ORIGIN: JAPAN

ENGINE: 998 CC

CYLINDERS: 4

MAXIMUM POWER: 179BHP AT 12,500 RPM

MAXIMUM TORQUE: 115.5 NM AT 10,000 RPM

GEARS: 6

DRY WEIGHT: 206 KG

MAXIMUM SPEED: 293 KM/H (182 MPH)

FUEL TANK CAPACITY: 18 LITRES

COLOURS: CADMIUM YELLOW, RAVEN/CANDY RED, PEARL WHITE/ RAPID RED, TEAM YAMAHA BLUE/ WHITE

COST: £13,399

Honda CBR1100XX Blackbird

The Japanese company Honda wanted to design the fastest motorcycle ever. In 1996, it created the Blackbird, named after the Lockheed SR-71 aircraft, another record holder. With a few tweaks, the Blackbird could rocket to an incredible 320 km/h (200 mph). In 1999, Suzuki stole Honda's thunder with the Hayabusa (see pp.58-59).

DID YOU KNOW?

In 2001, a rider on a turbo-charged Blackbird did a wheelie at an amazing 320 km/h (200 mph)!

The Blackbird had linked brakes. When the rider pulled the front brake lever the back brake worked, too. The back brake pedal also controlled the front brake pedal.

The Honda CBR900RR Fireblade was smaller, lighter, and faster than the Blackbird. It could go from 0 to 160 km/h (100 mph) in 6 seconds.

Thanks to its streamlined shape and huge engine, this bike could race from 0 to 209 km/h (130 mph) in 11 seconds.

STATS & FACTS

LAUNCHED: 1996

ORIGIN: JAPAN

ENGINE: 1,137 CC

CYLINDERS: 4

MAXIMUM POWER: 164 BHP AT 9,200 RPM

MAXIMUM TORQUE: 116 NM AT 7,300 RPM

GEARS: 6

DRY WEIGHT: 223 KG

MAXIMUM SPEED: 320 KM/H (200 MPH)

FUEL TANK CAPACITY: 24 LITRES

COLOURS: BLACK, BLUE, RED

COST: £10,500

Aprilia RSV Mille R

The Italian company Aprilia first became known as a maker of bicycles. In 1968, it began producing motorcycles and mopeds. In 2002, Aprilia launched the Mille R. This beautiful machine was big, fast and very comfortable. The 'R' stands for racing, since this bike was the fastest machine Aprilia ever made.

DID YOU KNOW?

'Mille' means 'one thousand' in Italian. The RSV was called Mille because the engine was almost 1,000 cc.

Until 2001, all Mille Rs were single-seat bikes. In 2002, Aprilia made a two-seater version.

One of the most eye-catching features of the Aprilia was its triple headlight.

STATS & FACTS

LAUNCHED: 2002

ORIGIN: ITALY

ENGINE: 997.6 CC

CYLINDERS: 2

MAXIMUM POWER: 128 BHP AT 9,500 RPM

MAXIMUM TORQUE: 101 NM AT 7,400 RPM

GEARS: 6

DRY WEIGHT: 168 KG

MAXIMUM SPEED: 270.4 KM/H (168 MPH)

FUEL TANK CAPACITY: 18 LITRES

COLOURS: APRILIA BLACK OR FLASHY YELLOW

COST: £9,999

The Mille had special radial brakes at the front. These were extra strong, so the bike could stop very quickly.

Triumph Daytona 955i

The Triumph Daytona 955i is a sport bike manufactured by Triumph from 1997 to 2006. It was powered by a 955 cc liquid-cooled, 3-cylinder, 4-stroke engine. The bike was launched in 1997 as the Triumph T595 Daytona and renamed Triumph Daytona 955i in 1999.

The Triumph was powerful, but also heavy. It weighed 20 kg more than the Honda Fireblade.

DID YOU KNOW?

A Daytona was featured in *Mission Impossible 2*, which starred Tom Cruise.

This is the Triumph Speed-Twin. It was first made in 1937 and continued to be made for over 20 years.

The Daytona had a 'naked' brother called the Speed Triple. It had the same engine and chassis, but no fairing.

STATS & FACTS

LAUNCHED: 1997

ORIGIN: UK

ENGINE: 955 CC

CYLINDERS: 3

MAXIMUM POWER: 147 BHP AT 10,700 RPM

MAXIMUM TORQUE: 100 NM AT 8,200 RPM

GEARS: 6

DRY WEIGHT: 191 KG

MAXIMUM SPEED: 265.5 KM/H (165 MPH)

FUEL TANK CAPACITY: 21 LITRES

COLOURS: JET BLACK, ACIDIC YELLOW, TORNADO RED

COST: £8,799

On the Water

Meet the record holders of the sea, in all shapes and forms, from the massive *Stena Discovery* which can ferry 1,500 passengers and almost 400 cars at great speed thanks to its four gas turbine engines, to the superfast California Quake Drag Boat, the first racing boat to achieve ¼ mile in under 5 seconds. No less impressive is *Illbruck Challenge* which sails round the globe battling waves, howling gales, collisions with icebergs and whales, powered only by the wind and the sheer determination of its crew.

Yamaha FZR WaveRunner

A combination of motorcycle, water ski and snow mobile, the WaveRunner can surge across waves at great speeds. It was the first sit-down watercraft designed for stand-up riding.

Thanks to nanotechnology, the WaveRunner has stronger hulls, decks and liners that are 25 per cent lighter than previous models.

DID YOU KNOW?

The telescopic steering column makes it easy for riders to go from sitting to standing, with three different riding positions.

DID YOU KNOW?

Yet more unusual facts bound to surprise you. Who would have thought that the nuclear-powered *Nimitz*-Class Aircraft Carrier could go 20 years without refuelling and last for 50 years? And there's more...

Riders perform amazing turns, jumps and loops. They can even dive completely under the water!

STATS & FACTS

All key data at your fingertips, to help you compare engine, size, weight and speed of the kings of the sea. Get on board and test the water!

The keel shape is designed for high-speed, supertight turning. Large pump inlet ducts provide great pickup.

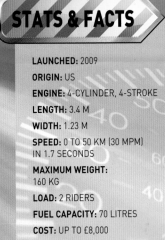

STATS & FACTS

LAUNCHED: 2009

ORIGIN: US

ENGINE: 4-CYLINDER, 4-STROKE

LENGTH: 3.4 M

WIDTH: 1.23 M

SPEED: 0 TO 50 KM (30 MPM) IN 1.7 SECONDS

MAXIMUM WEIGHT: 160 KG

LOAD: 2 RIDERS

FUEL CAPACITY: 70 LITRES

COST: UP TO £8,000

83

Stena Discovery HSS Ferry

Stena HSS ferries (High-speed Sea Service) are high-speed car carriers. They are catamarans, which means they have two hulls instead of one. The design makes for a smooth, speedy ride.

DID YOU KNOW?

Most car ferries are 'Ro-Ro' – roll (drive) on and roll (drive) off. In the past, cranes lifted each car on and off the boats.

The hulls are made from aluminium, which is light and does not rust.

Ferries operate worldwide.
This one serves the
Caribbean and can hold 200
cars and 1,000 passengers.
It has lounge areas where
passengers can relax
during the crossing.

Four massive gas turbine
engines produce as much
power as 600 car engines.

STATS & FACTS

LAUNCHED: 1997

ORIGIN: FINLAND

ENGINES: TWO GE LM2500 GAS
TURBINES, GENERATING 20,500
KW (27,490 HP) EACH, AND TWO
GE LM1600 GAS TURBINES,
PRODUCING 13,500 KW
(18,103 HP) EACH

LENGTH: 126.5 M

WIDTH: 40 M

MAXIMUM SPEED: 40 KNOTS
(74 KM/H / 46 MPH)

MAXIMUM WEIGHT: 1,500 TONNES

LOAD: 1,500 PASSENGERS
AND 375 CARS

FUEL CAPACITY: 10,000 LITRES

COST: £65 MILLION

Illbruck Racing Yacht

Inspired by the Whitbread Round the World Race and called the 'Everest of sailing', the Volvo Ocean Race has taken place every three years since 2001. The nine-month race covers 59,500 km (37,000 miles). The first winner was *Illbruck Challenge*.

Crews pull the cables for the sails using high-speed winches with long handles. The tallest mast is 26 m.

DID YOU KNOW?

The original race was inspired by the great seafarers who sailed the world's oceans aboard square-rigged clipper ships more than a century ago.

Round-the-world yachts
battle giant waves,
howling gales, collisions
with icebergs and
whales – and each other!

The satellite communications
centre contains telephone, email
and video transmission facilities.

STATS & FACTS

LAUNCHED: 2001

ORIGIN: GERMANY

ENGINES: N/A

LENGTH: 19.5 M

WIDTH: 5.25 M

MAXIMUM SPEED: 36.75 KNOTS
(67.6 KM/H / 42 MPH)

MAXIMUM WEIGHT: 13.5 TONNES

LOAD: 12 PEOPLE

COST: £16 MILLION

Atlantic 75 Lifeboat

The Atlantic 75 is a Rigid Inflatable Lifeboat (RIB) used to rescue people in trouble up to 80 km (50 miles) out to sea. It has a glass-reinforced plastic hull topped by an inflatable tube called a sponson. The latest version of this boat is the Atlantic 85 Lifeboat.

The hull and sponson are divided into compartments. If one section is pierced, the boat will not sink.

DID YOU KNOW?

If the boat capsizes, the crew inflates an airbag. The boat then turns the right way up in seconds.

The first rigid-hull inflatable lifeboat was designed by the British-based Royal National Lifeboat Institution in the early 1960s. These boats are now used worldwide.

The outboard motors are immersion-proofed so if the boat capsizes they are not damaged.

STATS & FACTS

LAUNCHED: 1992

ORIGIN: UK

MAXIMUM POWER: 2 X 70 BHP

LENGTH: 7.5 M

HEIGHT: 50 CM

MAXIMUM SPEED: 32 KNOTS (60 KM/H / 37 MPH)

FUEL CAPACITY: 181 LITRES

MAXIMUM LOAD: 500 KG

WEIGHT: 1.4 TONNES

ENDURANCE: 3 HOURS AT MAXIMUM SPEED

CREW: 3

Yamaha FZR WaveRunner

A combination of motorcycle, water ski and snow mobile, the WaveRunner can surge across waves at great speeds. It was the first sit-down watercraft designed for stand-up riding.

Thanks to nanotechnology, the WaveRunner has stronger hulls, decks and liners that are 25 per cent lighter than previous models.

DID YOU KNOW?

The telescopic steering column makes it easy for riders to go from sitting to standing, with three different riding positions.

Riders perform amazing turns, jumps and loops. They can even dive completely under the water!

The keel shape is designed for high-speed, supertight turning. Large pump inlet ducts provide great pickup.

STATS & FACTS

LAUNCHED: 2009

ORIGIN: US

ENGINE: 4-CYLINDER, 4-STROKE

LENGTH: 3.4 M

WIDTH: 1.23 M

SPEED: 0 TO 50 KM (30 MPM) IN 1.7 SECONDS

MAXIMUM WEIGHT: 160 KG

LOAD: 2 RIDERS

FUEL CAPACITY: 70 LITRES

COST: UP TO £8,000

Fire Dart Fireboat

The Fire Dart is a firefighting boat that patrols the River Thames in London. It is one of the lightest and quickest fireboats ever built.

DID YOU KNOW?

The Fire Dart can stop in about 14 metres.

Two massive engines provide more than 700 bhp!

Fireboats and firefighting tugboats tackle fires on board ships. There is never a danger that they will run out of water because they take their water from the river or sea.

A jet called a deck monitor shoots water in a stream over a fire. The rescue boat releases 475 gallons (1,800 liters) per minute.

OWNER No 3081

REG No 4768

STATS & FACTS

LAUNCHED: 1999

ORIGIN: UK

MAXIMUM POWER: 2 X 365 BHP

LENGTH: 14.10 M

WIDTH: 4.2 M

HEIGHT: 3 M

MAXIMUM SPEED: 30 KNOTS (56 KM/H / 30 MPH)

FUEL CAPACITY: 4,000 LITRES

MAXIMUM LOAD: 1.2 TONNES

WEIGHT: 6.1 TONNES

RANGE: 160 KM (100 MILES)

CREW: 4 CREW, PLUS 5 FIREFIGHTERS

Trent-Type Lifeboat

Every sailor fears shipwreck and drowning at sea. Brave lifeboat crews are always ready for rescue missions, even in the worst storms. Powerful Trent-type lifeboats are run by Britain's RNLI (Royal National Lifeboat Institution).

The survivor's cabin holds ten people. On board there are also heaters, dry clothes and a small galley.

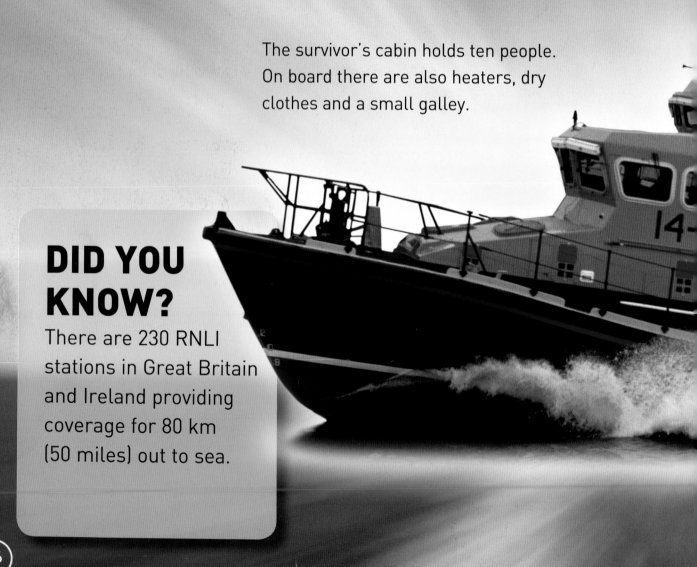

DID YOU KNOW?

There are 230 RNLI stations in Great Britain and Ireland providing coverage for 80 km (50 miles) out to sea.

Radar and radio equipment track ships in distress using the Marsat and Sarsat emergency satellite navigation systems.

The hull is made of plastic, carbon fibre and composites. These materials are light, strong and never rust.

STATS & FACTS

LAUNCHED: 1994

ORIGIN: UNITED KINGDOM

ENGINES: TWO-MAN DIESELS, 808 HP PER ENGINE, EACH ABOUT AS POWERFUL AS A FORMULA 1 RACING CAR ENGINE

LENGTH: 14.26 M

MAXIMUM SPEED: 25 KNOTS (47 KM/H / 29 MPH)

MAXIMUM WEIGHT: 27.5 TONNES

LOAD: 6 CREW, PLUS 10 SURVIVORS

FUEL CAPACITY: 4,100 LITRES

COST: £1.2 MILLION

Marine Protector

This is a Marine Protector Class US Coast Guard patrol boat. It is a fast, strong boat that can operate in rough seas. It is used to stop drug smugglers and chase other criminals. It is also used for search and rescue missions.

The pilot house is equipped with satellite navigation and autopilot.

DID YOU KNOW?

Each of the 73 boats in the US Coast Guard fleet is named after a marine predator. Names include *Marlin*, *Stingray* and *Mako*.

U.S. COAST GUARD

A small diesel-powered boat is kept at the back of the patrol boat. It is launched and recovered on a specially designed ramp. Only one person is required on deck for launch and recovery.

In America and the UK this boat is called a cutter. Cutters are boats that are more than 20 metres long.

STATS & FACTS

LAUNCHED: 1998

ORIGIN: US

MAXIMUM POWER: 5,360 BHP

LENGTH: 26.5 M

WIDTH: 5.18 M

MAXIMUM SPEED: 25 KNOTS (45 KM/H / 28 MPH)

FUEL CAPACITY: 11,000 LITRES

MAXIMUM WEIGHT: 92.4 TONNES

TOWING CAPABILITY: 200 TONNES

SURVIVOR CAPACITY: 10

RANGE: 1,445 KM (900 MILES)

ENDURANCE: 5 DAYS

CREW: 10

Deep Flight I Submersible

Submersibles are miniature submarines used for deep-sea exploration. *DeepFlight I* is a tiny one-person submersible with short wings that allow it to 'fly' through the water.

Lightweight material is strong enough to resist the tremendous pressure of the deep.

DID YOU KNOW?

In 2012, filmmaker and ocean explorer James Cameron reached the deepest point in the ocean – the Mariana Trench – in a custom-built one-man submersible. He descended almost 11 km (7 miles).

A submersible has the layout of a plane. Unlike a plane, however, the stubby wings pull the craft down through the water, rather than up off the ground.

DeepFlight I is equipped with six lights, which are needed because the bottom of the ocean is totally dark.

STATS & FACTS

LAUNCHED: 1996

ORIGIN: US

ENGINES: TWO MOTORS POWERED BY TEN 12-VOLT, LEAD-ACID BATTERIES, GENERATING 5 HP EACH

LENGTH: 4 M

WIDTH: 2.4 M

MAXIMUM SPEED: 12 KNOTS (22.2 KM/H / 13.8 MPH)

MAXIMUM WEIGHT: 3 TONNES

ASCENT RATE: 198 M PER MINUTE

DESCENT RATE: 150 M PER MINUTE

MAXIMUM DEPTH: NEWER *DEEPFLIGHT CHALLENGER* WILL REACH 11 KM

LOAD: 1 PILOT

COST: £1 MILLION (IN 2009)

Glossary

ACCELERATION The act of making a vehicle go faster using the accelerator pedal.

AERODYNAMIC A shape that cuts through the air around it.

AFTERBURNER System that injects extra fuel into the exhaust gases of a plane to provide large amounts of extra power.

AIR REFUELLING Method of refuelling military aircraft while in flight, via a fuel hose linked to a tanker aircraft.

ALUMINIUM A lightweight, strong metal that does not rust.

AUTOPILOT System that operates a vehicle without a pilot.

BHP Brake horse power, the measure of an engine's power output.

BODY Main part of a vehicle that houses the driver and passengers.

BOOSTERS Large canisters containing fuel that are attached to the sides of a space rocket as it is launched.

BRAKES Part of a vehicle used to slow it down.

CABIN A room in a ship used as living quarters by an officer or passenger, or the part of a plane that houses the crew and passengers.

CAPSIZE When a boat turns over in the water.

CARBON/GLASS FIBRE A modern strong, but lightweight material.

CATAMARAN A boat or ship with two hulls that are joined together by a wide deck or decks over the top.

CC Cubic capacity, the measurement used for the size of an engine.

CHASSIS The part that holds the engine, wheels and body together.

COCKPIT The part of an aircraft with the pilot and his assistants.

COMPOSITE A material or substance that is made of a mixture of materials, such as plastic, metal and fibreglass. Composites are usually very light and strong.

CUTTER A boat more than 20 m (65 feet) long.

CYLINDER The part of the engine where fuel is burned to make energy.

DECK MONITOR Water jet on a fireboat that shoots water high into the air.

DECKS The main floors or stories of a ship and especially the uppermost flat area where people walk.

EJECTION SEAT A seat, usually installed in military aircraft, that can be fired or ejected from the aircraft.

ENGINE The part of a plane where fuel is burned to create energy.

EXHAUST Pipe at the back of a motor vehicle that lets out poisonous gases made when petrol is burned. In some cases it is also used to reduce engine noise.

FAIRING Part of the bike covering the engine whose function is to produce a smooth outline so the motorcyle goes faster.

FIRE RETARDANT Liquid dropped onto fires to stop them from spreading.

FOREPLANES Movable surfaces at the front of a plane that provide extra lift and balance.

FORMULA ONE Famous car racing championship.

FOUR-WHEEL DRIVE A car that has power delivered to all four wheels.

FRAME The part of the bike that holds the engine, wheels and bodywork together. Also called the chassis.

FUSELAGE See Cabin.

GEARS System that lets a vehicle change speed without harming the engine.

GEAR-SHIFT PADDLES Levers on a steering wheel used to shift gears up and down.

HEADLIGHT The bright light at the front of the bike or car.

HORSEPOWER (HP) The measure of an engine's power, originally based on the power of an engine compared to a horse.

HULL The lower part of a boat or ship.

HYPERSONIC Able to reach speeds of Mach 5 and above.

IMMERSION-PROOFED Protected from water damage.

INFLATABLE A small rubber boat or raft filled with air.

JET Stream of fluid forced out under pressure from a narrow opening or nozzle.

JETS Part of an engine that provides the lifting power for an aircraft.

KNOT One nautical mile per hour, equal to 1.85 kilometres per hour or 1.15 miles per hour.

LASER-GUIDED BOMB A bomb launched from an aircraft that has sensors in its nose to guide it onto a target.

LINKED BRAKES System where the front brake lever also works the back brake, and the back brake lever works the front brake.

MACH Measurement that relates the speed of an aircraft to the speed of sound. Mach 1 is the speed of sound; Mach 2 is twice the speed of sound.

MAST A tall pole on a ship that may hold up sails, radio antennas, radar dishes or even flags.

MONITOR A mounted water cannon that throws powerful jets of water at a fire.

NANOTECHNOLOGY The science of using materials on a molecular scale, especially to create microscopic devices.

NOSE The rounded front of an aircraft or the front end of a car.

NOZZLE The end of a hose. Different nozzle attachments result in different water sprays, from a mist to a continuous stream.

ORBITER A spacecraft or satellite designed to orbit a planet or other body without landing on it.

PARACHUTE A large canopy with a body harness underneath. It is designed to slow the rate of descent of a person from an aircraft.

PILOT A person qualified to fly an aircraft or spaceship.

PILOT HOUSE Part of a ship where the pilot and the controls are based.

PROPELLER A machine with spinning blades that provides thrust to lift an aircraft.

PUMP A machine that raises or lifts a liquid or gas.

RADAR A method of detecting distant objects using radio waves.

RADIAL BRAKES Braking system where the brake discs are mounted at the bottom of the forks, parallel to the wheel.

RIGGED A ship equipped with sails and the ropes and chains used to control them.

RIGID HULL INFLATABLE BOAT Boat with a plastic hull topped by an inflatable tube called a sponson.

ROLL CAGE A metal framework in a car or racing boat to limit the damage if it turns over in an accident.

ROTOR Spinning blade.

RPM Revolutions (revs) of the engine per minute.

SAILS Fabric spread to catch or deflect the wind as a means of propelling a ship or boat.

SATELLITE NAVIGATION A system that tells you where you are and gives you directions by using satellites in space.

SCRAMJET A hydrogen-fuelled engine designed for flying at five times the speed of sound.

SENSORS Devices that help pilots fly their aircraft, detect enemy aircraft or fire weapons accurately.

SPOILER A lightweight panel attached to a car to prevent the vehicle from lifting up at high speeds.

SPONSON An air-filled tube that helps stabilise a boat on the water.

SPORTS BIKE A fast motorcycle that has been developed for road use.

STEALTH TECHNOLOGY Technology used to make a plane almost invisible.

STEEL Very strong alloy usually made by combining iron with carbon.

SUBMARINE See submersible.

SUBMERSIBLE A boat that can function under water.

SUBSONIC Slower than the speed of sound.

SUPERBIKE A fast motorcycle that is very similar to a racing motorcycle.

SUPERCAR A high-performance, high-cost production car.

SUPERSONIC Faster than the speed of sound.

SUSPENSION Springs and shock absorbers attached to a vehicle's wheels, intended to ensure a smooth ride even when travelling on bumpy surfaces.

TAIL The rear of the car or the rear part of the fuselage that balances a plane.

TANK A large container used to store fuel.

THROTTLE The part of a bike that is used to make it go faster or slower.

THRUST A pushing force created in a jet engine or rocket that gives aircraft enough speed to take off.

TITANIUM ALLOY A light, strong and heat-tolerant material.

TORQUE AND NM The measurements for an engine's power.

TUG A powerful boat that pulls or pushes ships.

TURBINE Machine with a wheel or rotor driven by water, steam or gases.

TURBO System that increases a motor vehicle's power by forcing more air into the engine.

TURBOFAN An engine with a fan used to boost its power.

TYRE A rubber covering for a wheel, filled with compressed air.

V/INLINE/FLAT The arrangement of the cylinders in the engine.

V8/V12 The engine size given in number of cylinders.

VALVE Device that controls the flow of petrol into the engine.

VIFF Vectoring in Forward Flight. A system that lets a plane change direction very suddenly.

VTOL Vertical Take-off, Vertical Landing. System that holds an aircraft in the air as it takes off or lands.

WINCH The method of lifting something by winding a line around a spool.

WINGS Part of the aircraft that provides lift, placed on each side of the fuselage.

WINGSPAN The distance between the tips of the wings of an aircraft.

Index

Index